That First Client

**How Purpose-Driven Entrepreneurs Can Find and Attract
Their First Ideal Client**

Jill Celeste, MA

Founder of the Celestial Marketing Academy

Copyright © 2016 Jill Celeste
Celestial Publishing

ISBN: 0692735666
ISBN-13: 978-0692735664

Cover designed by Vikiana
Author's photo by Jaimi Weatherspoon

Printed in the *United States of America*

DEDICATION

To my father, William John Hauver, Sr.

CONTENTS

ACKNOWLEDGMENTS

It takes a village to write a book. I am forever indebted to the following people who helped me on this journey:

Fabienne Fredrickson for throwing down the challenge,
Jen Levitz and Lori Hardegree for encouraging me,
and
My husband Richard for his unwavering support and love.

1. GETTING THAT FIRST CLIENT

Ask any established purpose-driven entrepreneur, and she'll tell you that getting her first client was one of the hardest obstacles she had to overcome.

For any new business, getting that first client is a challenge, but when you're purpose-driven, heart-centric entrepreneur, it is even *more* of a challenge.

First, you're a giver. You are more likely to give away your gifts than charge someone for them.

And while you are an expert in your craft, you haven't learned the marketing principles you need to get clients.

When you mix an inherent giving spirit with a lack of practical marketing knowledge, it spells disaster for the purpose-driven entrepreneur. Honestly, it's a recipe for business failure.

And we can't have your business fail because the world needs your gifts.

The world needs *you*.

So, it's time to change your mindset.

1) You must commit from now on to never give away your gifts for free.

2) You must commit to learn the marketing fundamentals you need to find and attract clients.

Which means you now have a new job title:

You are the Director of Marketing for your business.

Yes, the Director of Marketing. And it's the most important hat you wear as an entrepreneur. Why? Because marketing is how you'll get that first client (and the second, and the third). The other tasks – the ones that have nothing to do with marketing – such as managing your email, emptying your office trash, and balancing your books – are not going to help you get that first client. Only marketing does.

I can't express how important these mindset shifts are for the success of your business.

Now, let's get on to what's in this book…

This book is a 100-percent, no-holds-barred, non-frivolous guide to finding and getting your first client. Each chapter will take you through the steps you need to follow to attract that first client. You will have assignments too. Some of these assignments can be completed right in this book, while others can be downloaded from my special Resource Page (www.ThatFirstClientResources.com).

Reading this book will help you. No doubt. But doing the work assigned to you from each chapter will help you even more. In fact, doing the work is what will make you more successful. So, think of this book as a textbook, and your final exam will be your implementation of each assignment, culminating to your ultimate test of all: Getting that first client.

One more thing before I delve into the content:

You can do this.

That first client is not as elusive as you think.

You are unique and wonderful and talented, and the world is blessed that you're here.

I am blessed that you're reading this book (thank you).

I believe in you.

I am rooting for you.

I love you.

Let's get started, shall we?

2. WHO ARE YOU MEANT TO SERVE

"Everyone is not your customer." – Seth Godin

It's time to identify who it is you want to serve. You see, we are not just looking for any old first client; we are looking for the most wonderful, most ideal person to be your first client.

In order to do that, you must know who your ideal client is.

If marketing was a long line of dominos, knowing who your ideal client is the first domino that must fall. Everything else in your marketing strategy relies upon knowing this information.

So, who are meant to serve? Let's find out.

Who Is Your Ideal Client?

Every entrepreneur has an ideal client – *but so many entrepreneurs have no idea who their ideal client is.* And that's a mistake (a huge mistake, in fact).

Why?

Because everything you do in your business is intended for your ideal client. And if you don't know who your ideal clients are, then how do you know if your products are the best for them? Or if your marketing copy is speaking to them? Or that you're using the right social media sites to reach them?

You don't. You are taking a stab in the dark. And stabs in the dark do not make successful businesses.

Stabs in the dark, in fact, lead to failures.

And I don't want you to fail.

Now that you know how important *knowing* who your ideal client is, let's look at how you can pinpoint identifying *yours*:

Look at your own journey

Many times, especially if you're a new entrepreneur, *your ideal client is a version of you.*

A client has three stages to her journey: *The before, the transformation and the after.* She is in the "before" state when she meets you, and when she is done working with you (the transformation), she's in her desired "after" state.

Many entrepreneurs have undergone these same journeys, and their businesses are based on these transformations. While you are now in the desired "after" state, examine what your life was like before you made the transformation.

ASSIGNMENT: Answer these questions to help you reflect upon your own journey:

- Why was I stuck in this "before" state?

_____

_____

_____

_____

- What issues or problems was I experiencing?

_____

_____

_____

_____

- What was keeping me up at night?

_____

_____

_____

_____

- What motivated me to look for a transformation?

_____

_____

_____

• How did I feel once I made this transformation?

_____

_____

_____

_____

Ask your ideal clients

Sometimes, you know someone who is your ideal client, even if you haven't worked with her yet. This may be someone you met through networking or someone in your peer group.

If you know a person who is your ideal client, then ask her to fill in the blanks for you. You can do this through a simple email. Tell the recipient you are trying to find more ideal clients – just like her – and ask if she could answer a few questions for you. You can type the questions right in your email, or link to a survey (SurveyMonkey.com is a great tool for this). Most people are happy to help, especially if you keep it short and sweet.

ASSIGNMENT: Head over to www.ThatFirstClientResources.com to download a sample email you can send to your ideal client. Feel free to use it verbatim, or shift the language so it's in your voice.

Demographics and Psychographics

Now that you have a general idea on who your ideal client is, you need to drill down even more. It's time to delve deep into the demographics and psychographics of your ideal clients.

In case these are new terms to you, here are their definitions:

- *Demographics* are the features of a specific population, such as age and location.
- *Psychographics* are the behavioral and lifestyle features of a specific population, such as interests and opinions.

If you're a visual learner, check out this table to help understand the differences between demographics and psychographics:

Demographics	Psychographics
Gender	Interests
Age	Attitudes
Income	Opinions
Location	Biggest struggle or problem
Marital Status	Hobbies
Profession	Lifestyle

Look back at the research you've already gathered about your ideal client. Analyze this information and organize the data into demographics and psychographics. If you followed the email sample I provided on the Resources page, you will have this information on hand. Don't hesitate to ask your ideal clients to fill in any holes.

As you meet more people – and learn more about your ideal client – your knowledge about her demographics and psychographics will grow. Keep a running list to help you keep track of what you've learned.

ASSIGNMENT: Document the demographics and psychographics of your ideal client in the table below.

Demographics	Psychographics

Creating Your Ideal Client Persona

Once you determine the psychographics and demographics of your ideal client, create an Ideal Client Persona. In other words, you are creating a profile, or a client avatar, that is the perfect representation of your client.

Here is the flow you can follow when writing your Ideal Client Persona:

1) Start by naming your ideal client. As hokey as it sounds, naming your persona helps others identify with it (because it seems like a real person who is just like her).
2) Consider buying a stock image to add to your persona – some type of photographic representation of your ideal client (make sure the photo matches the demographics of your ideal client).
3) Describe who your ideal client is and what her biggest problems are.
4) Isolate what your ideal client needs to do to solve her problems.

Remember: The idea behind writing an Ideal Client Persona is to get your perspective client to say "This is me!"

It may take you several revisions to finalize your Ideal Client Persona – but do not give up! In fact, as long as you're in business, you will be tweaking – and maybe revamping – your Ideal Client Persona. It is normal!

Take time to interview your ideal clients to learn the *exact language* they are using to describe themselves. This will help you write an Ideal Client Persona that will make people want to work with you.

ASSIGNMENT: It's time to write your Ideal Client Persona. Fire up Microsoft Word and start typing. Head over to www.ThatFirstClientResources.com to see examples of other entrepreneurs' ideal clients.

Mastering The Marketing Pull Question

Now that you have your Ideal Client Persona written, it's time to learn how to write marketing pull questions.

Marketing pull questions are questions you ask in your marketing copy that *pull your ideal clients to you.* It focuses on your ideal clients' struggles and problems, and helps them realize that you understand their predicament.

One more thing: When reading your pull questions, the answer that should always pop into your ideal client's mind is YES.

And with some practice and a good Ideal Client Persona, marketing pull questions are not too difficult to write.

Here's what to think of when writing your pull questions:

- Spell out clearly what is your customer's problem today (not yesterday's problem, or tomorrow's problem)

- Make it one idea and focus on one thing

- Stick to one sentence for this question

- Use words that evoke emotion and feeling

- Be simple and clear (this is not the time for SAT prep words!)

- Use words your ideal client says

(See how your Ideal Client Persona will help you with your marketing pull questions? The questions are already spelled out in the persona!)

Here are three pull question examples to get your creative juices flowing:

- Did you have high hopes on working out this morning but you decided to stay in bed instead?

- Have you promised to stop yelling at your kids only to find yourself screaming at them during homework time?

- Do you want to learn more about Twitter but haven't found the time to even start your account?

To kick your pull questions up a notch, think about creating an image that pops into your reader's mind. In other words, paint a picture for your reader that reminds her of her life right now.

Check out these examples and see how they conjure up an image in your mind's eye:

- Do you often stare at the produce section in the grocery store, wishing your kids would eat more fruits and vegetables (then end up throwing more Little Debbie snacks into your cart)?

- Are you at the breaking point of your business where you've thought about quitting and going back to the corporate world, and even though the very thought of it makes you want to vomit?

- Do you wake up at 2am in a cold sweat because you're worrying (again) about how you will find people to buy your products?

- Have you been desperately trying to find clients for your business to the point you'll take *anyone*, even people who underpay but overwork you?

Why are these sentences even more powerful?

First, they use *actions words*, such as stare, wish, throw, quit, vomit, worry, underpay and overwork. Secondly, they *create a setting* – a sense of place for your ideal client (grocery store, corporate world, middle of the night in bed).

Your goal when writing your marketing pull questions is to kick it up a notch. Write the best marketing pull questions you can.

Be patient with the writing process

Ernest Hemingway once said: "The first draft of anything is shit."

It's important to remember that writing is a process. Even the most gifted writers in the world write drafts after drafts until they reach a point of satisfaction. Expect to write several drafts of your pull questions. Once you complete one draft, step away from it for a while and then look at it with fresh eyes.

Did you know Stephen King puts first drafts of his books in a drawer and doesn't look at them for six weeks?

You probably don't have the luxury of waiting six weeks, but you can come back to your writing in a few hours or even the next day. The idea is to step away, gain perspective and come back to your writing.

ASSIGNMENT: Draft 5-10 pull questions that you can use in your marketing. Conjure up an image in your reader's mind, and make sure the answer to each question is YES.

1. _____

_____

2. _____

_____

3. _____

_____

4. _____

_____

5. _____

_____

6. _____

_____

7. _____

_____

8. _____

_____

9. _____

_____

10. _____

_____

Once you have written your marketing pull questions, think about how you can incorporate them into your marketing. Here are some ideas:

- Homepage of your website
- Business card
- Elevator speech
- Marketing collateral (flyers, brochures)
- Speeches and presentations

3. TELLING THE WORLD WHO YOUR IDEAL CLIENT IS

"People influence people. Nothing influences people more than a recommendation from a trusted friend. A trusted referral influences people more than the best broadcast message. A trusted referral is the Holy Grail of advertising." – Mark Zuckerberg

Now that you have nailed down your Ideal Client Persona and marketing pull questions, it's time to tell everyone about who want to serve through your business.

And, I mean…*everyone*.

This chapter is all about asking for referrals. For some purpose-driven entrepreneurs, asking for referrals can be hard because you do not want to impose upon your friends and families. You may even have an independent streak.

It's time to push this mindset to the side. You can still be true to your authentic self and ask for referrals. Let's learn how…

If you're an entrepreneur, you must master the art of asking for a referral. That's because referrals are one of the fastest ways to get your first client – and any new clients thereafter.

In fact, your business should *always* focus on getting referrals, even when you're at full capacity. It's an inexpensive and highly effective way to attract clients.

So, how do you get referrals for your business? Check out these four steps:

#1: Finding possible referral sources

So, who are your referral sources? Honestly, they can be anywhere! Start by making a list of who you know. Here's a list to get your creative juices flowing:

- Family

- Friends

- Social media contacts

- Former work colleagues

- Networking peers

- High school friends

- College friends

- Alumni associations

- Places of worship

- Neighbors

- Past clients

- Sales prospects

- Vendors

- PTA

- Youth sports/activities

- Community service

- Business schools/marketing academies

At first, you want to reach out to everyone you know. You just don't know who the PTA president knows! As you move along in this process, you can start segmenting your list. (Check out the book, *The Referral of a Lifetime*, by Tim Templeton for great information on segmenting your referral list).

ASSIGNMENT: Who are your referral sources? Jot down some ideas in the spaces below.

_____

_____

_____

_____

_____

_____

_____

_____

_____

#2: How to ask for referrals

Now that you have a list of referral sources, here are some ways you can approach them for referrals:

1) **Letter:** This is when you send a letter – through snail mail – to your referral sources to let them know about your business and to ask for referrals. We'll delve into this later in this chapter.

2) **Coffee Dates:** As you network, you will meet certain people who seem like the "networking mayors." They know everyone and are natural connectors. Ask these influencers to meet you for coffee to learn how you can refer business to them, and how they can refer business to you.

3) **JV Partnerships:** These are more formal arrangements. Think about other entrepreneurs who have the same ideal clients as you, but you service them in other ways. For example, if you're a wedding photographer, potential JV partners could be florists, wedding planners, and DJs.

#3: What to share with your referral partners

You don't want your referral partners to have to guess *one thing* about your business. You must supply them with the right information so they can refer your ideal clients to you. Here's what you want to share:

- Who you want to work with (your ideal clients)

- How someone can reach you

- What locations you serve

- What types of programs/services you offer

Think about putting this information in writing so that your referral partner has it at hand to refer to later. Even something as simple as giving your referral source a dozen of your business cards can help her easily refer people to you.

#4: Thanking your referral source

How will you thank your referral partners for their referrals? Even if the referral doesn't pan out, you still want to thank her.

For example, you may decide to send a thank you note and a gift card for a successful referral, but if the referral didn't work out, you can send a card and follow up with an email to explain what happened.

This is important for two reasons:

1) People like to *feel appreciated*, and you'll increase the likelihood that you'll get more referrals.

2) If someone doesn't pan out, it gives you an opportunity to *further educate your referral sources about your ideal clients and business* – so that he can send an even better referral to you in the future.

Never forget the thank you part! Planning for it now will make it more automatic for you when it occurs (because it will!).

ASSIGNMENT: Who are people you can meet for coffee dates? Who are potential JV partners? Brainstorm some ideas in the spaces below.

_____

_____

_____

_____

_____

_____

_____

Your Ideal Client Persona...Everywhere!

While your Ideal Client Persona is a great internal exercise, it's not something you want to keep a secret. In fact, it's essential that you post your Ideal Client Persona everywhere. It will help your ideal clients identify themselves, as well as help your referral partners send you potential customers.

So, how can you get your Ideal Client Persona everywhere? Here are some ideas:

Post your Ideal Client Persona on your website

Do not skip this step! When people find your website, make it super easy for your ideal clients to read your persona and self-select. Remember, the idea of the Ideal Client Persona is for your target audience to read it and say "This is me!" So, make it front and center on your website.

There are multiple ways to do this. You can link to it from the top navigation. Or, you can have it right on your homepage. If you have multiple ideal clients, you can have a button for each one on your homepage, and send your visitors to internal pages for more information.

ASSIGNMENT: Go to www.ThatFirstClientResources.com to see examples of how to add the Ideal Client Persona to your website.

Make an Ideal Client flyer

You can easily convert your Ideal Client Persona into a one-page flyer. Open up Microsoft Word, paste your logo in the header, and insert the copy for your Ideal Client Persona right into the Word document. You can then convert it to a PDF that can be easily emailed to your contacts, as well as posted to your website.

Make sure to have your Ideal Client Persona flyers printed out as well. Bring them to your networking meetings. Share with your audience when you give a presentation. Include them in a letter and mail to your contacts. It's a valuable piece of marketing collateral!

ASSIGNMENT: Go to www.ThatFirstClientResources.com to see an example of an Ideal Client Persona flyer – and then make sure to create your own!

Make a condensed version of your Ideal Client Persona

Step back from your Ideal Client Persona and think about how you can summarize it in one to two sentences. This is critical for inclusion in:

- Your elevator speech
- Your video intros
- Your business cards
- Your bio
- Social media accounts

ASSIGNMENT: Write a one- to two-sentence "condensed" version of your Ideal Client Persona. Use the blanks below to brainstorm, and then circle the one you want to use in your marketing.

_____

_____

_____

_____

_____

_____

_____

_____

The Power of Snail Mail

When was the last time you mailed a letter? Believe it or not, "snail mail" is an effective marketing tactic, especially if you do it consistently.

You may be thinking: *Mailing letters? That is so old school!*

I know. It *is* old school, but think about this:

1) Have you ever *not* opened a personal letter? Now consider: How many emails do you delete *before* even reading them?
2) How many times have you *skimmed* a long email? Now consider: How many times have you read, and *then reread*, a long letter?
3) How excited are you to receive an email from someone? Now consider: How *surprised* (and then excited) are you to get a letter in the mail from someone?

Do you see how mailed letters are more likely to get someone's attention?

And that's why letters are the perfect tactic for asking for referrals!

Here are some tips to help you get your first letter mailed:

Give thought to the paper and envelope

Take time to pick out the right paper and envelope. Ideally, do not use copy paper and white standard envelopes. Consider stationery that attracts the eye and makes you look professional. For a greater impact, get personalized stationery on high-quality paper.

Schedule your letters and consistently mail them

These "asking for referrals" letters work best when done consistently. Think of your letter-writing efforts as a campaign, and get out your calendar to plan accordingly. What topic will you cover in your letters? What days will you mail them?

Equally important, commit to your schedule. You're in the spotlight now, so make sure to follow through on your promise to mail regularly (ideally once a month).

Mail a letter to everyone

If you have a mailing address, then that person should receive your letter. *Don't be shy!* One of the best ways to collect addresses is through Postable.com. You can send a link to everyone on your email list or through social media, asking your contacts to add their mailing addresses to your Postable account.

Make it personal

This is not the time for being generic! Make each letter personal. Write it in such a way that the person feels like you are talking to him. And if you are comfortable doing so, add personal information to your letter, such as what your kids are up to, or a vacation you are planning.

Sending letters to all of your contacts is a great way to acquaint people with your company, and, ultimately generate referrals and sales. Even in our modern age of technology, people still love to receive "snail mail." Take advantage of the personal aspects of letter writing, and you can spread your marketing message in a more intimate way to people.

ASSIGNMENT: Go to www.ThatFirstClientResources.com to see a sample letter you can mail for your referral campaign. Then, write your letter and mail it to everyone you can. Plan how you will mail these letters every month. Use a calendar to help you.

Telling Your Email Contacts

Snail mail is awesome, but sometimes you can't mail a letter – and that's when it's time to email your contacts.

A word of caution: Don't email your contacts in lieu of "snail mailing" them. Snail mail first, then email.

So, what should you say in your email? *Here's a checklist to help you:*

- ☐ Explain that you are looking to expand your business (or you just started your business)
- ☐ Identify the type of ideal clients you are looking to work with
- ☐ Ask her if she knows anyone who is your ideal client
- ☐ Try to arrange a phone meeting or coffee date with your contact to discuss your business and ideal client more, and if your contact is a fellow entrepreneur, express your desire to learn more about her business
- ☐ Ask that she confirms receipt of the email and to email you back with ideas

Keep the email short and sweet – and get right to the point. You are looking for referrals. Your brevity will be appreciated by your email contact.

One more thing: If you have anything that you can attach to your email (such as a flyer with your Ideal Client Persona), feel free to include this in your email. Don't make your email contact guess who to refer to you!

ASSIGNMENT: Draft a message you can email to your contacts. Make a list of who you can contact and start emailing. Don't forget to keep track of their responses (which is especially helpful if you need to follow up with anyone).

4. CONTACTING FUTURE CLIENTS

Follow up and follow through until the task is completed, the prize won. – Brian Tracy

You've told everyone who your ideal client is, you've mailed out your warm letters – and now you're getting the attention of people you can serve.

So, how do you convert these sales leads into clients?

This is the part that vexes most purpose-driven entrepreneurs. You don't want to be a pushy salesperson. You don't want to pressure anyone. You just want them to know you are here for them when they need you. However, you can't be passive in your sales process if you want clients.

Good news! You can have an effective sales process that doesn't make you feel icky. Ready to learn how?

I Would Love To Work With You!

Chances are, as you told people you were building a business, someone said: "Oh, I would love to work with you!"

Now is the time to contact these potential sales prospects to let them know you are open for business!

This is a crucial first step in getting people into your pipeline.

And don't just rely on email for this initial message. The best way to tell people you're open for business is through a phone call.

Yes, the good, old-fashioned telephone…

(You can do it!).

Before images of telemarketers pop in your head, here's what you need to know: You are not asking for their purchase during this call. Instead, you're inviting them to learn more about your services through an Introductory Sales Call. So, call everyone who has expressed an interest with you and let them know your business is open. Then, invite your sales prospect to a free Introductory Sales Call so you can learn more about their struggles and how you can help. This is when you will share your packages and pricing as well.

Save the selling and wooing for the Introductory Sales Call, okay? Your goal here is to get these people on your calendar so they can learn more about working with you.

ASSIGNMENT: Get out a piece of paper (or fire up Microsoft Word), and make a list of everyone who has expressed even the smallest interest in working with you. Make sure to include these people's phone numbers on your list too. Hang on to this list because you'll need it later in this chapter when I teach you more about the Introductory Sales Call Process.

Your Introductory Sales Call Process

You've reached out to people who've expressed an interest in working with you, and you have Introductory Sales Calls on your calendar. Woo hoo!

Before you have your first Introductory Sales Call, it's important to establish a process for these calls. This will help you stay confident through the process, and your ideal client will love the flow and energy that this process brings.

Let's take a look at the steps you can follow to create your introductory sales call process:

#1: Create a pre-call questionnaire

Before you speak on the phone with your interested sales prospect, you want to have her answer a few questions. This can be accomplished through a short pre-call questionnaire. You can create this questionnaire through SurveyMonkey.com or a similar tool, or you can just type the questions in the email and ask that she email her responses to you. Be firm that you need her responses back at least 24 hours before your scheduled call. This shows her level of commitment to getting the help she needs, plus you'll have time to evaluate her responses.

Try to keep the questionnaire as short as possible. My pre-call questionnaire is only five questions. It's not an intake form – it's just a way to see what she needs and if you can help.

Here are the questions I ask on my pre-call questionnaire (to inspire your own questions):

1) First name, last name, and email
2) Please explain your current business. Why do you do? Services? Typical clients?
3) What are you currently doing to market your business?
4) What obstacles, challenges, and struggles do you regularly come up against?

5) What would you like to see happening 12 months from today (realistic goals, but a bit of a stretch)?

ASSIGNMENT: Go to www.ThatFirstClientResources.com and look for my sample pre-call questionnaire. Feel free to model it for your own!

#2: Email testimonials before the call

You want your sales prospect to see your client results before your call. So, collect any testimonials you have received and put them on your website. That way, you can email a link to your Testimonials page to your sales prospect.

Don't have any testimonials yet? No worries – use your LinkedIn recommendations or online reviews left for your business. If you've done work for clients without charging them, contact them to get testimonials.

As you get more clients, you'll get more testimonials, and you can add them to your Testimonials page to share with future sales prospects.

#3: Prepare your sales call script

Most introductory sales calls are only 30 minutes long, and you have a lot of details to go over. That's why you want to write your pre-call script before you get on the phone with your sales prospect.

Now, purpose-driven entrepreneurs like you and me are often uncomfortable with the sales process, and we don't want to come off as a high-pressure, icky sales person on the phone call. You may even think that creating a sales script will make you look too sales-y and shy away from writing one.

However, the opposite is true! Having a sales script ready for your Introductory Sales Calls helps you stay authentic while keeping you comfortable as you offer your services to your ideal client.

So, what should go in your script?

Here's the beauty of that pre-call questionnaire because you will repurpose it for your sales script! Chances are your sales prospect put down an answer, but you need to do more probing. So, go through each question on your pre-call questionnaire and ask the sales prospect to go a little deeper. Take great notes during your call. You want to constantly summarize what your sales prospect is saying so that she knows you are listening to her – and she hears (again) why she needs your help.

Once you've gone through these questions, it's time to decide: Can I help this person? If the answer in your mind is yes, you want to ask for the sale.

Simply ask: *After listening to your current situation – your struggles and issues – and the goals you want to achieve, I am confident I can help you. Would you like to hear more about my services?*

If she says yes, then go over your services and pricing. Ask for her permission to go to the next step (e.g. *Which package sounds the most interesting to you? Would you like the price for XYZ package?*).

Once she has this information, including the pricing, your next question is *It sounds like the XYZ package is the perfect fit for you. So, the ball's in your court. What do you think? Are you ready to take the leap?*

ASSIGNMENT: Go to www.ThatFirstClientResources.com to see a sample call script that you can model – and make sure to write your own!

#4: Create follow-up steps

When you hang up the phone, your next step is to go into follow-up mode.

If your sales prospect said yes, then it's time to bring her on board.

If your sales prospect said, *no/not yet/I need more time to think about it,* then you want to add her to your Follow-Up List, which I will talk about next.

Your Introductory Sales Call Process is one you'll perfect with practice. Take imperfect action and implement what's been outlined here, and then refine it as you learn more about your sales prospects and what resonates with them. With each new sales call, you'll get better and better – and more confident offering your services to your ideal clients.

Make A Follow-Up List

Most of your sales prospects will not purchase from you after your first meeting or phone call. In general, only two percent of sales occur at the first meeting. Here's another important fact: Most people won't commit to purchasing from you until after you followed up *at least five times*.

That's why you need to have a sales follow-up list.

Now, I am not talking about a collection of Post-It Notes or handwritten notes stuffed in a manila folder somewhere. I am talking about a real, tangible, bona fide list of people you need to follow up with.

Your follow-up list is critical to your business. In fact, it's one of the most important documents you'll create for your business. This is a list of people you can serve and help – and a list of people who will pay you so you can continue to serve others with your gifts.

So, how do you make a sales follow-up list? Here are some steps to get you started:

#1: Designing your follow-up list

As corny as it sounds, I believe in designing a gorgeous follow-up list. These are my people, my tribe, those who I am meant to serve, and I want to honor them accordingly. So, I tend to use colors and nice paper. I like to have a positive energy around my follow-up list, which for me, translates to color.

You may have another way of honoring the people on your list. It's completely individualized. What I want you to take away from this lesson is that you don't want to haphazardly put a list together. You want to design a format that's appealing to you.

Let's say you're like me and like colors. You will be much more energized to look at your follow-up list if it's colorful and not some bland spreadsheet. On the flip side, maybe you like crisp and modern-looking documents. Again, you'll be much more inclined to look at your follow-up list if you design it to match your personal tastes.

So, draw hearts, use that fancy fountain pen, fill in rows with color, print on resume paper – whatever works for you. Design a follow-up list that makes you excited to look at it.

#2: Include all names on your follow-up list

Many purpose-driven entrepreneurs don't want to "hound" their ideal clients during the sales process. Furthermore, you don't want to pester people who you are not 100 percent sure want to work with you.

This is a self-defeating mindset – something you must overcome to get your first client.

Your follow-up list is a list of anyone who has ever expressed an interest in working with you. *Anyone.*

If you met someone at a networking meeting who said "Oh, I would love to hire someone like you," then her name goes on your follow-up list. If your friend says her cousin could use your services, then your friend's cousin goes on your follow-up list. If you had an introductory sales call with someone, that person goes on your follow-up list. And when you get former clients, they'll go on your follow-up list too.

Ask yourself this question: *Who has expressed – even in the smallest way – an interest in working with me?*

Anyone who pops into your head as a response to this question should be included on your follow-up list. Don't talk yourself out of including a name on your list. *Include everyone.*

#3: Other details to include on your follow-up list

Your follow-up list is exactly that – *your list.* The other details you want to include are up to you. Most entrepreneurs include the sales prospect's contact information, such as an email address or phone number.

Here are some other details to consider:

- How you met this person
- Programs she has purchased from you already
- The date you last contacted her
- How you reached out to her last (phone call, email, small gift)

Because you will probably reach out to this person multiple times, I would definitely track your contact history. *How did you reach out to her? When did you last reach out to her?* That way, if you want to vary your follow-up methods, you'll know how you contacted her in the past.

#3: Where to store your follow-up list

Here's a mistake I have made in the past: I created this beautiful follow-up list, put in a gorgeous folder and then filed it away. And that's where it stayed until I come across it, looking for something else.

The truth is that your follow-up list must be in front of you at all times. Otherwise, you run the risk of never looking at it once you create it.

So, stick it under your keyboard, pin it front and center on your bulletin board, place it on a clipboard next to your laptop – wherever it makes sense for you. Just make sure it is always visible.

In Chapter 6, I will give you come ideas on how to create a follow-up process.

Until then, remember this: *Your sales follow-up list is precious*. It contains people you can serve. It's a map for increasing your income. It's a critical document for your business. Do not half-heartedly complete this task. Put your whole heart into designing your follow-up list. Commit to touching base with everyone you can serve. When you do this, you'll get that first client – and more clients in the future.

5. STEP AWAY FROM YOUR COMPUTER

You can just sit there and wait for people to give you that golden dream.
You've got to get out there and make it happen for yourself.
– Diana Ross

I get it. There's stuff to do that requires your computer: Facebook updates, blog posts, emailing prospective clients...

But here's the truth: If you never step away from your computer, it will take you longer to get that first client.

A lot longer...

You have to step away from your computer – and do so strategically with visibility-enhancing activities that will work like a beacon, showing your ideal client the way to you.

Let's take a look at two of the biggest, best and most effective "non-computer" activities you can commit to: networking and public speaking.

Your First Client Is Probably Someone You Will Meet In Person

Now that you have some marketing fundamentals down, *it's time to step away from your computer and go find your ideal clients.*

Here's the reality: Your first ideal client is probably someone you will meet in person.

Think about this way: Would you be more likely to purchase from someone you've met personally or someone (a stranger, in fact) you've met online?

Even in our highly digital world, nothing beats an in-person connection. It's the fast track for getting your ideal client to know, like and trust you.

And to my fellow introverts: I get you. I am not a fan of networking and Chamber mixers either. I understand how utterly exhausting in-person interactions are. It sucks the life out of you.

Planning is your friend, fellow introvert. Know it will be a mentally taxing day. Add buffer time to your calendar so you can recuperate. Schedule in your nap afterwards.

Tough love? Introversion cannot be a crutch. You have to embrace how you are, plan your schedule accordingly, and step away from your computer to find that first client.

I had to do it, and I promise you, you can do it too.

Networking

One of the best ways to meet your first client is to attend in-person networking meetings. Networking meetings are not only great ways to find customers, but they also help you build an "unpaid sales force" of people who can refer business to you.

How to find networking groups

Finding the right networking groups is a bit like shoe shopping; You have to try some on before you find the perfect fit.

To help you start your research, here are some ideas on where you can find networking groups:

- Google networking groups in your area (make sure to include your town/city in the search, such as "networking groups Dallas" or "women's networking groups Miami")
- Check out MeetUp.com
- Research if any professional organizations meet in your area
- Ask other entrepreneurs where they network
- See if there's a local alumni group for your college
- Start your own

ASSIGNMENT: It's time to research local networking groups! Find some groups and add their dates to your calendar so you can plan to attend.

Know who attends the meeting

If you are attending a networking meeting for the first time, do some homework about the people who normally attend these meetings. This is best accomplished by "interviewing" the president or founder of the networking group. Ask her how many people attend the meeting, what professions they represent and the number of referrals the group members give each other. This will give you a good feel for the type of people you will be networking with (and if it's worth your time to even attend the meeting).

How many group should you belong to

The whole point of networking is to increase your visibility. Truth be told: If you don't have clients, then you have time to network. At first, try out as many networking groups as you can.

At a bare minimum, you want to attend one weekly networking meeting and 2-3 monthly networking meetings.

Remember: Your first client is out there somewhere! The more you network, the greater the chance you'll find her.

Have a perfect business card

Your business card is not a collateral piece to be taken lightly. Make sure you have a business card with your photo, contact information and marketing pull questions to entice people to learn more about your business.

Also, don't be afraid to give a card to a person more than once. Many times someone will have misplaced your first card.

Finally, keep a box of business cards in the glove compartment in your car. That way, you will never run out!

ASSIGNMENT: Need help designing the perfect business card? Go to www.ThatFirstClientResources.com for tips on how to design a business card that is like a mini-billboard for your business.

Master your elevator speech

Your elevator speech (also called a 30-second commercial) is a powerful tool in your networking arsenal, so be sure to be prepared by having your speech ready prior to your networking meeting. Also, consider having variations of your elevator speech, especially if you attend a networking group on a weekly basis (this way, you will give the networking attendees something new to hear about your business).

A quick Google search will give you numerous formulas for an elevator speech. Find one that works best for your style. Just make sure you include your first and last name, as well as web address, and repeat both pieces of information at the end of your elevator speech. People need to hear things several times before retaining it.

ASSIGNMENT: Head over to www.ThatFirstClientResources.com for tips on writing your elevator speech.

Prepare how you'll greet someone you haven't met before

You've heard the saying: *You only have one chance to make a good first impression.* That is especially true at networking events. When approached by someone you have not met before (or if you approach someone), be ready for how you will strike up the conversation. The best tip is to get the person to speak about himself, so ask what he does for a living and what challenges he experiences in his business. Be ready to identify how you may be able to assist this person, or be a "bridge" and help make a connection between two networking group members who could benefit from knowing each other. Making introductions makes you instantly memorable.

The point of networking is about visibility for your business. The more networking events you attend, the more people you meet, the greater your visibility. This all translates to a better chance of meeting that first client!

Speaking

In addition to networking, getting speaking opportunities – whether at a local networking group or by hosting your own workshop – will help you find that first client.

Right now, you may not feel confident about your public speaking skills (and that's okay!). *Here are some tips to help you:*

Rehearse and rehearse again

One of the reasons why people are so nervous about public speaking is because they are afraid they will forget what they want to say. That's why it is essential to rehearse your speech multiple times before you present.

Consider rehearsing in front of a mirror, or better yet, record yourself with your smartphone or tablet. If you feel even braver, do a test run with a friend or family member. Not only are these good ways to get feedback, but it will also help you get comfortable with others watching you.

Don't be afraid to use index cards

I once attended a wedding where the sister-in-law delivered the wedding toast by reading it from index cards. She had rehearsed it, but she had her cards there to help her. And you know what? There was nothing wrong with it!

A successful speech doesn't always mean a memorized speech.

Index cards are a speaker's best friend. Use them to help you deliver everything from your elevator speech to your signature talk. No one will think less of you for using them!

Admit you are nervous

Depending on where you are presenting – and who you are presenting to

– it may be okay to "spill the beans" about your nervousness. Most people get nervous before they speak, and showing your vulnerability will make you resonate with most of your audience. And sometimes, confession is good for the soul. If you profess that you're nervous, you can push past it and get on with your content.

Join Toastmasters

Toastmasters International is a membership organization with meetings around the world. It helps people learn how to perfect public speaking. Members review your presentations and provide honest feedback in a safe environment. They help you learn communication skills and take you through the steps you need to be a good public speaker. Check out their meeting location tool to find a meeting near you.

Hire a voice coach

Many of the top speakers in the world hire voice coaches to help them be better public speakers. A voice coach will help you develop a great-sounding voice, build confidence about your voice and body language, and improve your sentence structure, diction, and language. They can also help you get over any nervousness you have about public speaking. Hiring a voice coach is a great investment for speakers of any comfort level.

While you're fine tuning your public speaking skills, it's time to find places where you can be a guest speaker. *If you need ideas, here are some places to start looking:*

- Your own networking groups
- Networking groups that you're not a member of (many accept outside speakers)
- Professional organizations
- Chambers of Commerce
- Podcasts
- Webinars
- Livestreaming shows

ASSIGNMENT: Where can you speak? Brainstorm a list of possible places where you can be a guest speaker:

_____

_____

_____

_____

_____

_____

_____

_____

_____

_____

Once you get a commitment to speak, it's important to have a client attraction process in place for your speaking engagements. *Here are some steps to consider:*

#1: Determine your requirements before committing to speak

Think about what you want in advance before you agree to speak. This could include a minimum number of audience members, a requirement for people to provide their email addresses to add to your list or a written plan on how they'll promote your talk. A best practice is to put your questions into a survey that you can share with someone who asks about your speaking services.

Establishing some ground rules prior to a speaking commitment will help ensure you are setting yourself up for the best event possible - *one with your ideal clients in attendance.*

#2: Your speech should be the what and why - but not the how

When creating your content, you want to give your audience the "what" and "why" of your topic. You don't want to give them the "how." Save the "how" for your coaching programs or company services. This will whet your audience's appetite to learn more, and they will be more eager to schedule a follow-up call with you.

ASSIGNMENT: It's time to come up with some speech topics! Think about the biggest questions you get from your clients, Use your marketing pull questions for inspiration too. In the spaces below, brainstorm some ideas on what you might speak about:

_____

_____

_____

_____

_____

_____

_____

_____

_____

_____

_____

_____

_____

#3: Identify how you'll document your audience's information

Here's what I do: I offer a raffle (usually a low-cost gift card to a local restaurant or coffee shop), and the audience members fill out a raffle form. On this form, I ask for their contact information, if they want free Introductory Sales Call, and if they want to be added to my email list. It's just a half-page form, but I get great results from it.

ASSIGNMENT: Go to www.ThatFirstClientResources.com for a sample raffle form you can download.

#4: Have a follow-up process

Once you return home from your speaking gig, go through your raffle forms (or give them to your VA). Send out emails to everyone who asked for an Introductory Sales Call, and make sure to add people to your Follow-Up List. Then, enter in those names who have opted into your mailing lists.

Don't procrastinate on these tasks! Creating a system is essential. I do these tasks as soon as I get home from every speaking gig. Another tip: If you use a customer management software, make sure to tag each person with the event name. This will help you trace where you are getting your referrals from.

One final word: Don't just show up to speak. Make sure you are capitalizing on every speaking engagement, and use it as a tremendous opportunity to add people to your list and to schedule Introductory Sales Calls. It's how you may find that first client!

6.   FOLLOWING UP WITH LOVE

Success comes from taking the initiative and following up...persisting...eloquently expressing the depth of your love.
– Tony Robbins

You have your Sales Follow-Up List that you created in Chapter 4.

Now, don't do what many entrepreneurs do. They make the list and never do a thing with it.

No, no, no!

You've heard the expression, "the magic is in the follow-up." And it's true.

Tough love, okay? You have to follow up. You have to persist. But you can do it all with love. Let's read how.

Creating A Powerful (But Loving) Follow-Up Sales Process

I'll be the first to admit: *I am not comfortable with the entire sales process.* It's a necessary part of building my business, though, so I am coming to terms with selling my services. Here's how I am adjusting my "salesperson" mindset:

First, I needed to accept my discomfort with selling. Then, I had to accept that selling is just a means for people to get the marketing help they need. Finally, I focused in on the parts of the selling process that makes me feel the "ickiest."

And for me, I feel the most "icky" when I am following up with my sales prospects. So, to help combat these feelings, I created a powerful *but loving* follow-up sales process that may help you too.

#1: Take excellent notes during your Introductory Sales Calls

Here's why this is so important: Your notes can help guide your follow up. If you do your Introductory Sales Calls properly, you'll learn about your prospect's struggles, goals and pain points. This is great information to use when you follow up. (Keep reading to see what I mean).

#2: Set up a time every week for following up

To make following up with sales prospects a priority, **block time on your calendar every week.** I add it as an appointment on my calendar, and I hold this time as very sacred. In other words, don't book over it!

ASSIGNMENT: Go to your calendar right now and block times every week for you to do follow-up calls and emails.

#3: Set a reminder on who you need to follow up with

Each sales prospect may have a different frequency for when you follow up. For example, someone you just spoke with last week should be emailed today, while someone who's been on your follow-up list for months may only need to be contacted once every four weeks.

Therefore, it's important that you stay organized with who you need to follow up with and when. Again, use your calendar and Follow-Up List to help you here. On that week's appointment, write down who you need to follow up with.

The key is to set a reminder notification to help you remember who you are following up with on that certain day, which is why I like to add this information directly to my appointment.

#4: Vary your follow-up methods

Email is the most popular form of follow up (and one of my favorites). If you love to email, make sure you vary what you say. One email could include a link to a relevant article, and another email could be more conversational. This is where your Introductory Sales Call notes come in handy! Ask how your potential client is doing with their pain points, or if they've overcome a certain struggle yet. Make sure to be assuring that their issues are surmountable, and you'd be glad to help.

Don't forget to include your sales prospects on your mailing list for your e-newsletter; that's another excellent way to keep "top of mind" with your sales prospects (without being pushy).

I'll give you even more follow-up ideas later in this chapter.

#5: Just be yourself

To me, this is the most important part of the follow-up sales process. Recognize that "people love to buy but hate to be sold to" – and then be yourself as you approach each sales prospect. I tell my potential clients that I hate to sell and be pushy, and that I am just checking in because I have been thinking about them (all true words). Be yourself – whatever that looks like for you – and you'll feel more comfortable with the sales process.

Most salespeople will tell you that the magic is in the follow-up. That's because those who follow up consistently close more sales. I believe, however, that *the follow-up is magical because you get an opportunity to show that you care for your sales prospect and hope to help them.* While getting paid is part of the business, most purpose-driven entrepreneurs have an innate need to help people. Following up is how you show this purpose time and time again. Get comfortable with the follow-up process by automating your tasks, blocking your calendar and corresponding with authenticity. The more you follow up, the more comfortable you'll feel – and yes, the more sales you'll get.

How To Stay In Touch With Your Sales Prospects

Often, entrepreneurs will use email and phone calls to follow up with sales prospects. While there is nothing wrong with these methods, there are other ways you can stay in touch. Diversifying your approach often leads to better results!

Check out these four ways to stay in touch with your sales prospects:

#1: Send an article or tip that would be of interest to them

One time, I had a prospect who worked with authors, and I saw a media inquiry from HARO (Help A Reporter Out) that she could respond to. I emailed her the inquiry with directions on how to respond. *She was so appreciative!*

If you see a blog post, article or other item of interest, send it to your sales prospect. You can email it to her, or simply tag her name on social media. An even better idea would be to "snail mail" it to your prospect. As I mentioned earlier, people do not get much personal mail anymore, so you'll definitely stand out!

#2: Use an automated card delivery system

Sites such as Send Out Cards and Postable make it super easy for you to send greeting cards, gifts and postcards to your sales prospects. As I have mentioned already, people rarely get personal mail these days, so sending something in the mail is a great approach.

You can store your prospects' information on these websites (including birthdays and anniversaries). And the selection of cards ranges from inspiration to funny. Check them out for a great way to automate your "keep in touch" campaign.

#3: Use Amazon Prime and send small gifts

One of the best investments I make every year is Amazon Prime. Their free shipping option pays for itself. Consider sending your favorite book, or a journal, or other small gift to your prospects – right through Amazon. You can include a gift message, and they'll ship for you. It's easy, and you don't have to stand in line at the post office!

#4: Get her opinion on a new product or service

Want to make your sales prospect feel extra special? Ask her for her opinion on a new product or service you are creating. Including your sales prospect in your market research helps you in many ways. First, you'll get valuable feedback from your ideal client. Also, it's a great "touch point" between you and your sales prospect (without feeling too "sales-y"). Finally, being involved in the market research may pique your sales prospect's interest and encourage her to buy from you.

Think about how *you* want to be kept in touch with as someone's sales prospect. While you may be okay with "just checking in" emails and phone calls, how *delighted* would you feel about receiving a card in the mail, or being asked for your opinion on a product? You want your sales prospects to feel extra special.

ASSIGNMENT: Go to www.ThatFirstClientResources.com and download the "Following Up With Love" PDF. It's chock full of ideas on how you can follow up with your sales prospects, plus it includes some resources to help you with your following up.

7. RINSE AND REPEAT

We are what we repeatedly do. – Aristotle

You've learned about understanding who your ideal client is and how to tell the world about who you're meant to serve. You've also learned about how to contact future sales prospects and lovingly follow up with them. And you now understand that your first client is waiting for you – usually away from your computer.

In essence, you've learned the vital and basic marketing principles to get that first client.

And guess what? These principles don't change for your second client or your third client....

It's a matter of rinse and repeat. Ready to learn more?

Stay True To What Works

Until you are at full capacity with your business, the steps outlined in this book are what you need to follow every day to keep getting clients.

This will be hard, especially if you're like me and get distracted by shiny objects.

But I am here to tell you: The marketing techniques in *That First Client* are tried and true.

I use them to this day to get clients. My students use these techniques too (with great results!).

So, don't stray from the course. Stay true to what works, okay?

ASSIGNMENT: When you get your first client, I want you to email me so I can celebrate with you. I mean it! Here's where to send your email: CelestialMarketingAcademy@gmail.com. I will answer you (and celebrate with you) personally.

If you're a Twitter geek like me, you're welcome to tweet me @jill_celeste and tell me the good news.

I can't wait to hear about your successes!

You Need To Market Your Business Every Day

Before I end this book, I want to get on my soap box and drill home something very important.

You need to market your business every day.

Which means this:

Every day, you need to implement at least one thing from this book.

Why should you market every day? Here's a little quiz:

Question: What brings you customers?
Answer: Marketing.

Question: What helps you earn a profit?
Answer: Marketing.

Question: How do you reach the people you are meant to serve?
Answer: Marketing.

Notice the answer isn't being a slave to your email, or taking out the office trash, or balancing your books. The answer is *always* marketing.

Every day, you must market your business.

(That's what Directors of Marketing do!)

Experts say you should spend four hours a day marketing your business. How many hours are you marketing every day? If it's not around four hours, and you are not at full capacity, then it's time to make adjustments.

If this all sounds unfeasible, please allow me a moment of tough love:

Which would you prefer: Marketing every day – as many hours as it takes – or closing your business?

You have gifts to share with the world! We need you to be open for business!

So, if you don't have that first client or you need more clients, then it's time to rearrange how you are spending the day.

It's a mindset shift, yes, but a necessary one. I want you to be a success. I want you to embrace your role as Director of Marketing for your business. And I want you to market every day. I promise – it's the missing ingredient that you've been looking for to get that first client.

RESOURCES

There's only so much I could squeeze into this book. And the teacher in me wants to give you more, more and more.

That's why I created a special resource page to enhance the lessons and assignments from *That First Client*.

Head over to www.ThatFirstClientResources.com to see all the goodies I have for you.

Transparency notice: I will ask for your first name and email before giving you access to the Resource Page. This allows me to track who is getting the resources, as well as helps me build my email list. Nothing sleezy, I promise, but I like to be upfront about why I need your personal information (I would never spam you either - yuck!).

ABOUT THE CELESTIAL MARKETING ACADEMY

The Celestial Marketing Academy is an online marketing school specially designed for purpose-driven entrepreneurs with the following "Marketing Wish List:"

- I want to feel assured that I have figured out exactly how to best market my business
- I want to know what marketing tactics to implement to grow my business
- I need a plan that guides my marketing at all times (because I get so distracted!)
- I want to be a confident, knowledgeable Director of Marketing for my business
- I will demystify marketing – finally – and not have to guess at it anymore

If you're a purpose-driven, heart-centric entrepreneur (or want to be), you can learn more about the Celestial Marketing Academy at JillCeleste.com/Academy.

ABOUT JILL CELESTE

Jill Celeste, MA is a bestselling author, marketing teacher and founder of the Celestial Marketing Academy. Jill helps entrepreneurs learn how to market their businesses to attract more clients. Jill's coaching is unique because she helps entrepreneurs transform their cluttered, disorganized marketing into a strategy that helps them grow their businesses. Through coaching and online programs, Jill teaches her clients how to finally differentiate themselves in the marketplace so they can get new clients and make more money.

Jill graduated with a B.A. in English from Wesleyan College in Macon, Georgia. She obtained her master's degree in history from the State University of Georgia in Carrollton. Prior to becoming a marketing coach, Jill worked for 15 years in the private sector and has experience in marketing and public relations in healthcare, IT and small business.

Jill lives in Tampa, Florida, with her husband, two sons, three guinea pigs and a basset hound named Emma.

For more information about Jill's coaching programs, please visit JillCeleste.com.

Made in the USA
San Bernardino, CA
14 July 2016